Contributing Author
Dona Herweck Rice
(*Write All About It!* series)

Editor
Patricia Miriani Sima

Editorial Project Manager
Karen Goldfluss, M.S. Ed.

Editor in Chief
Sharon Coan, M.S. Ed.

Art Director
Elayne Roberts

Cover Artist
Larry Bauer

Imaging
Hillary Merriman

Product Manager
Phil Garcia

Publishers
Rachelle Cracchiolo, M.S. Ed.
Mary Dupuy Smith, M.S. Ed.

Us
Newspaper in the
Writing Process

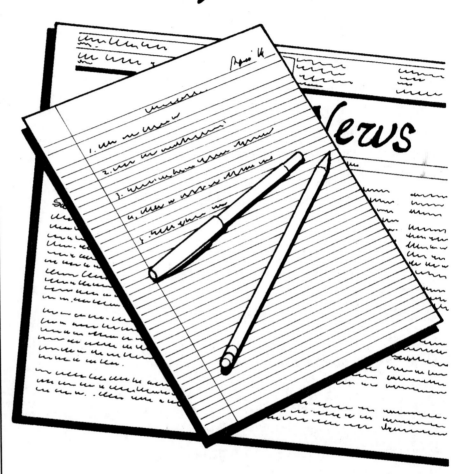

Author

Raymond Harris

Teacher Created Materials, Inc.
6421 Industry Way
Westminster, CA 92683
www.teachercreated.com

©*1996 Teacher Created Materials, Inc.*
Reprinted, 2004
Made in U.S.A.

ISBN-1-55734-479-5

Contents

How to Use this Book

What to Do

1. Read the short unit that precedes your assignment. Each unit focuses on a special skill: how to choose a subject, making plans for writing, gathering facts, and so on. The skills that you learn are not just "school" skills. These are skills you will use again and again throughout your life for all of the various kinds of writing you do in school, at home and in your chosen career. As you learn these skills, try to remember to use them as often as you can in all of your writing.

2. Read the instructions for your reading and writing assignments carefully. Each assignment involves both reading and writing. You will be able to choose the reading you do yourself, usually from your local newspaper. Then you are asked to do a writing assignment where you can use the skill that you learned about in the unit. If there is anything about the assignment you do not understand, ask your teacher, writing coach, editor, or your writing partner for help.

3. When you work on your assignments, work the way a newspaper reporter does. Newspaper reporters and other writers always write a rough copy first, then they revise it, polish it, and rewrite it before finishing their final work. You should do the same with the assignments in this book, and with everything else that you write for others to read.

What You Will Accomplish

➡ As you complete each assignment, you will prove to yourself that you can write better than you ever thought you could.

➡ You will learn and practice skills that will help you with all the writing you will ever do in school, at home, or in your chosen career.

➡ You will find that the more you write the easier it is to do.

➡ When writing becomes easier for you, you will find that it helps you to do better in all of your school subjects.

➡ You will find that you enjoy writing.

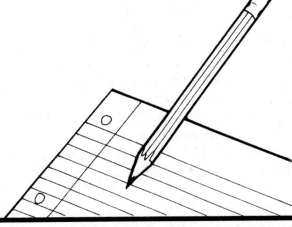

How to Use this Book (cont.)

The Order of the Units and a Word to Teachers

Writing teachers may choose to teach the units and assignments in the order they appear in the book, or they may prefer another order. For instance, many teachers feel that planning should be taught before choosing a subject. The units will work equally well either way. Because the habit of writing a rough draft is so important, some teachers may want to talk about this part of the writing process before the first writing assignment, and again when student writers are further along in the units.

Some units may be taught together instead of separately. The three units on "gathering facts," for example, may be discussed together. Teaching writing, like writing itself, is a very flexible process, and writing teachers are encouraged to use a unit order that is best suited to the needs of their special writers.

Reading and a writing assignments are provided throughout this book. They allow student writers to deal with the skill or the part of the writing process they have just learned. Reading and writing units are based on newspaper reading. Therefore, students should be encouraged to begin a regular newspaper reading habit.

Because writing must inevitably be integrated into one whole process, you may want your student writers to be working on a continuous, unified writing project at the same time that they are dealing with the shorter assignments in the units.

Unit 24 provides detailed directions on how to organize a classroom newspaper. Although this activity can be completed at any time, it would make an excellent culminating activity in which students can use skills acquired from the other units. This activity can be repeated throughout the year with students taking on different jobs each time.

Computer-assisted writing unquestionably makes the drafting, editing, and rewriting steps of the writing process worlds easier and more enjoyable for student writers. You are encouraged, therefore, to give your writers as much time with your school's computers as possible.

Writing Process Stages

☞ Pre-Writing

Activities that precede writing are vital to any successful writing program. A writer must activate his or her thought process and creativity before actually forming a draft. Some writers require more preparation than others, and the requirements will vary according to the topics. However, all writers benefit by this sort of beginning search. The pre-writing activities given here can be used on their own to build preparatory skills, or they can be utilized as the initial stages of a specific writing project.

☞ Writing

Through pre-writing, the author develops a store of information to use. Now writing is ready to begin. It is the step of the process where form takes place as information is filtered and shaped to meet the author's intentions. The ideas are made to connect for another audience. Writing calls for focus and structure—the narrowing of pre-writing generalities to specifics. However, content above mechanics is the prime concern. Activities that foster this approach can be found in this book.

☞ Response

It is sometimes difficult for a writer to know how another interprets what he has written. How helpful, then, to have an audience in the process of writing to aid the author in directing himself. This is done through reader response. The author can more readily get across what he intends by understanding the message the audience is receiving. Reader response can be managed in many ways. Peer response sheets, partner meetings, and writing circles are some of the best. Additionally, some activities simply lend themselves to response. Samples can be found in the response section included in this book.

☞ Editing

Editing and revision go hand-in-hand, although to distinguish (if that's necessary), an analogy can be made. If the writing was a car, revision would be handled by the design engineer and editing by the mechanic. One designs and shapes while the other repairs and maintains. An important thing for you, the teacher, to remember at this stage is that it is not your job to edit. Forget "correcting" student writing. Your job as teacher is to comment, give feedback, and eventually to evaluate and grade, but the piece and all of the steps of the process belong to the author.

☞ Revision

So often a child puts something on paper and is loathe to alter it in any way. She feels that if that word or mark is not there, it was a wasted effort. To that child, revising means fixing mistakes and recopying. Yet the child who has real ownership of the piece—awareness that her writing belongs to her and comes of her knowledge—will be as excited by the revision as by the writing. Revision is not slashing with red to see what's "wrong", but rather remolding to clairify exactly what one wants to say.

1 *Tips for the Writing Program*

- Include a daily writing period in your schedule. Set aside a writing center for conferencing and writing folder location.

- Writing time does not have to be silent time. Allow the students to collaborate. A small group, called a writing circle, often works best.

- Conferencing is essential. During writing time meet with a writing circle. Focus on one student's work at a time, allowing the others to observe and input as well. Let the author "run" the conference by talking through his/her own work. You will comment or question in order to guide, not direct. Often the best comment is "Tell me what you want to write about."

- Keep all work in a writing folder. Students can keep all writing and running lists of words and topics in their individual folders.

- Topic lists should consist of all considered topics; word lists should consist of any word that the student finds interesting, appealing, useful, or in any way worth considering for future use.

- Model and participate in all writing yourself. Let the students see the process in action— you'll be surprised at how much they'll teach you! The overhead projector is an excellent modeling tool.

- Use computers if possible. They lend a professional air and take the drudgery out of revision (as well as the belief that revision means recopying).

- Illustrations should always be encouraged.

- Display and publish various writings by various students. Store the writing as part of the classroom library.

- Share everything! Students need to write for an audience as well as to hear what others are saying.

- Never underestimate the power of a journal! Journal writing should be a daily event. Why not begin the day with a journal topic on the board and a five minute journal free write time (with optional sharing afterwards)? Teacher can write, too, or use the time to take care of classroom business and get the students focused at the same time. Word plays, puzzles, cartoons, and graphic designs can all be part of the journal. It's a place for individual creativity and expression—let them go!

What Is There to Write About?

Writing Focus...
Creating a List of Writing Ideas

When you ask the question, "What is there to write about?" it's like saying, "What is there to talk about?" Writing and talking are what you might call kissing cousins. They have the same family name—communication—and both writing and speaking work to the same end. They pass ideas about information from one person to another:

- "Hey! Were you at the game last night?"
  (This is something to talk about. A conversation has begun.)

- "The Celtics edged out the Knicks when a wobbly free-throw scored in the last two seconds of play."
  (This is something to write about. A sports story has begun.)

There is as much in this world to write about as there is to talk about. If you can talk about it, you can write about it.

Why, then, when you have a writing assignment to do, is it so hard to think of something to write about? Actually, it is also difficult to think of something to say when you are pressed to speak. What happens when someone says, "Let's talk"? It might go like this:

"What do you want to talk about?"

"I don't know."

"I don't know either."

Silence.

The best talking and the best writing ideas come when you are not being pushed to think of a subject. Ideas come in odd moments. Someone says something that reminds you of something you have thought about too. You read an article that gives you all sorts of things to think about. You may be angry or happy and want to express your feelings. You see or read something interesting and you want to share the experience with others.

But what do you do when you are told to write an article? "Write about anything at all," your writing coach says. Naturally, your mind goes blank. With all the things you have done in your life, with all the things you know about, you moan, "What is there to write about?"

The best thing to do is relax. Forget about it for a little while. Do not forget about it, exactly, but let the assignment cook on a back burner in your mind until the ideas start to simmer. Then start a systematic search for ideas. One way to do it is outlined in the summary box that follows the unit.

Searching for Writing Ideas

➡ Leaf through articles in newspapers and magazines.

➡ Skim through your textbook if the writing assignment relates to a school subject.

➡ Exchange ideas with friends.

➡ You may find ideas in pictures, songs, outdoor adventures, television, and radio.

➡ Jot down ideas as they come to you. Write down anything and everything. Good ideas are often bad ideas that have been changed a bit.

➡ Keep a journal, diary, or scrapbook. When you write notes to yourself on a regular basis you always have a fund of interesting ideas to draw upon.

➡ When you think you have an idea brewing, write a sentence or two about it. Scratch and scribble to your heart's content while you are searching for ideas. It doesn't have to be good or neat. Just get it down on paper where you can look at it and think about it.

Reading and Writing Assignment

A Great List of Writing Ideas

Suppose that you have been told to write an article about anything at all, and you do not know where to begin. Your first job is to think of an idea.

1. Browse through a newspaper or magazine to find ideas.

2. Jot down at least five ideas for topics you think you would like to write about. Write each idea in the form of a short sentence.

   Examples:

   ✓ The Chicago Cubs are contenders for the pennant this year.

   ✓ I disagree with the advice Ann Landers gave to a teenager.

   ✓ Why is disarmament a good (or bad) idea?

   ✓ There are good ways and bad ways to lose weight.

3. Look through a newspaper and make a list of at least 25 different topics that have been written about. Circle at least 5 in which you are interested.

How to Choose and Narrow Down a Subject

Writing Focus...
General versus Focused Subjects

Many times when you are given a writing assignment, the subject has been chosen for you in a way: Write an article about baseball; discuss the French Revolution; write about a famous person.

Even though you have been given a general subject to write about, you still have a long way to go in deciding exactly what you will write about. For example, you can not tell everything there is to know about baseball in one writing assignment. The French Revolution went on for years. What part of the French Revolution will you discuss? Of thousands of famous people, which one will you write about?

Your first job, then, is to narrow down the subject until you have it small enough to work on. One reason that beginning writers find it hard to fill up a page is that the subject is so large that they do not know where to begin. It is impossible to get organized and get started if you are going to try to cover the entire history of baseball, in two or three pages.

You decide to write about famous batters such as Ty Cobb, Babe Ruth, Lou Gehrig, Hank Greenberg, Willie Mays, Hank Aaron, and so on. This is still too much to write about easily. The subject needs even more narrowing.

Here are some possibilities: Compare the batting records of two great hitters.; Tell how Willie Mays hit 51 homers in 1951 and still had enough on the ball to hit 52 home runs ten years later.; Tell what you think about this year's choice for most valuable player. Now you have some subjects that are just a nice bite size, easy to handle and will be interesting to read.

One procedure you can follow when trying to choose and narrow down a subject is outlined in the summary on page 10.

Choosing and Narrowing a Subject

➡ After you have chosen a general subject, think about the subject or do some research to find out what part of the subject you would like to write about.

➡ Make a list of facts and ideas you may want to talk about.

➡ If there seems to be too much to talk about, narrow the subject some more by choosing one or two items from your list.

➡ A good rule is that the narrower and more specific your subject is, the easier it will be to write about, and the more interesting it will be for others to read. This is called finding a focus for your writing.

Reading and Writing Assignment

Finding a Focus for a Subject

1. Read a detailed feature article in your newspaper. A feature article is a prominent story in a newspaper that discusses a subject as well as reporting news about it. There may be features that discuss a health problem, something to do with government, the World Series, the Olympics, the environment, television, and so on.

2. After you have read the article, tell in a sentence or two:

   a) what the general subject is and,
   b) what part of the subject the writer has focused on.

3. Describe a general subject you would like to write about.

4. Tell what the focus of your article will be.

4 *Thinking and Planning*

Writing Focus...
Making Plans for Writing

There is very little you can do in this world without doing some thinking and planning first. And the more complicated a task is, the more thinking and planning it takes to do it well. Writing, like any other activity, calls for careful thinking and planning.

Thinking and planning begin when you first pick a subject, narrow it down, and find a focus for it. Then, you must plan how you will gather the facts and ideas that you will include in your writing.

You do more thinking and planning as you organize your facts and ideas. You have to decide what you will talk about first, second, and third. You have to think about which ideas you will explain in detail and which you will touch on lightly. You will think about how you want your writing to sound. Will it be serious or funny? Will it have an agreeable or a sarcastic tone? Will it be a simple statement of facts or will it include your personal opinions?

As you get on with your writing, the thinking and planning never stop. Which words will you choose? Is the original plan working or does it have to be changed? Is there a better way to say what you have said?

This may sound difficult and complicated. But it is much more difficult and complicated to try writing without a plan. Like a coach in a football game, you can always change your game plan. And good writers do change their plans as they go along. But you must start with a plan in mind, and it's best if the plan is written down.

Planning

➡ Your first planning consists of thinking about the subject. What do you already know about the subject? How can you find out more if you have to?

➡ Talk to others about your idea. Make notes about what you learn and about new ideas that are suggested.

➡ Try to get yourself psyched up for the project just like players psych themselves up before a game. You need to be interested and enthusiastic about what you are going to do in order to do it well.

➡ Make notes about your plans on a piece of paper. Your plans will probably change as you gather information, organize it, and start to write. That's fine. You do not want to throw your plans out the window, but always be aware that you need to work with a plan at every stage of your writing.

Making Plans for Writing

1. Read an article that deals with news from another part of the world.

2. Now, pretend that you are a reporter who has been assigned to write an article on a subject of world interest. Choose a different subject than the one you read about in the newspaper, or think about a different part of the same subject.

3. Decide what your subject will be, narrow it down, and decide on a focus.

4. Write a paragraph or make a list of steps that tells how you think you will go about writing this article.

Gathering Facts and Ideas By Reading

Writing Focus...
Finding and Using Research Sources

Many beginning writers think that all the ideas and facts they use in their writing must come straight out of their own heads. Not so. Most of the facts and ideas that writers use come from other writers!

This is not to say that everyone copies from everybody else. Most of the facts and ideas a writer needs have been written about before by someone else. What writers do is search for these facts and ideas and put them together in a new way to create a new information and new ideas.

Searching for ideas and information in the work of other writers is called research. Writers use many different sources for their research. These sources include newspapers, magazines, dictionaries, encyclopedias, atlases, books, library files, microfilm records, sound cassettes, computer data banks, pamphlets, manuals, and so on.

If you are asked to write about another country, for instance, there are a number of sources where you can gather information easily. A good place to start is an atlas or a general encyclopedia. Also check the card catalog in your library under the name of the country to see what books are available. If you have time, you can call or write a consulate or embassy of the country to ask for information.

Suppose you want to write about Norway. Without doing too much research you will find that thousands of books, pamphlets, and articles have been written about Norway. It saves time if you try to focus on one aspect of Norway when you do your planning—the fishing industry, the history of the country, winter sports, popular tourist attractions, etc. If you start with a foggy idea that you want to "read about Norway," you may spend the rest of your life in the library without getting through it all.

One of your best allies in finding reading material for your research is your librarian. Once again, when you ask for help, you should have focused and narrowed your subject as sharply as possible so that the librarian knows where to direct you. Librarians not only can tell you what is available in the library; they can also tell you where to look or where to write for additional information.

Make notes as you read. Do not copy everything, just the facts and ideas that apply to your narrowed subject. Keep track of where each idea and fact comes from. Sometimes you want to go back for a second look.

Gathering Facts by Reading

➠ Be sure you have narrowed your subject enough so that you have a pretty good idea of what you are looking for.

➠ When you do your planning, make a list of places you might go to get information.

➠ Use the library. Ask the librarian for help.

➠ Make notes.

➠ CAUTION! Writers do not copy facts and ideas word for word. Writers gather facts and information, and then use what they have read to express their own ideas in their own words.

Reading and Writing Assignment

Finding and Using Research Sources

1. Find and read an article in your newspaper about some aspect of science, technology, or medicine. Tell in a sentence or two what the article is about.

2. Write a few sentences that tell what kind of information the writer may have had to find by reading.

3. Make a list of at least three reading sources where you might be able to find facts and ideas about this same topic, if you had to write this article yourself.

4. **Optional:**

   a. Write an article that deals with the same subject you read about in the newspaper article.

   b. Try to provide new facts or ideas that are not in the article you read.

   c. At the end of your article, list the reading you did to find the information you used.

6

Gathering Facts and Ideas By Observing

Writing Focus...
Making Notes from Observations

Some of the most famous writing in the world has come about through reporting what the author has seen. One of the most famous is *The Origin of Species* by Charlie Darwin, where the author proposed a revolutionary theory about the development of life forms on earth by observing plants and animals all over the world.

On a more modest scale, every newspaper has its outdoor writers who report on birds, gardening, wildlife, hunting, fishing, and sports of all kinds. Much of this reporting is done by observing what is happening and writing about it.

This doesn't mean to say that no reading or research is involved in this kind of writing. Before observing the activities of wildlife, for example, writers should become informed about what they are going to see. You cannot write a very good article by observing eagles, let's say, if you know nothing about eagles except that they fly. Nor can you write a complete article about a basketball game without having done some reading beforehand to find out about the players, the team standings, and so on.

As you plan your writing think about the things you may want to learn from your observations. Make notes or a list of things you want to see. For example, you have read that eagles build nests or "aeries" in the top of a tree. You want to see where such a tree is located and how the nest is built, if that is possible to see through your binoculars. Or, perhaps you can see an aerie in a museum of natural science.

Take notes as you make your observations just as you take notes when you read. As you watch something, you not only gather information, your feelings are affected as well. This may be important in your writing. How does it feel to see the huge nest an eagle builds? What does the majestic head and glowering eyes of an eagle make you think of?

It is even a good idea to write a few sentences about your experience while you make your observations so that you do not forget how you felt at the time. Some writers take a recorder along so that they can make spoken notes as they observe. Important points are reviewed later and written down.

Gathering Information By Observing

➡ Become familiar with your subject by reading about it.

➡ In the planning stage of your article, think about the things you may want to learn from your observations.

➡ Take careful notes as you watch. Write down ideas and feelings you have as well as factual information.

➡ Write some rough sentences and paragraphs as soon after making your observations as possible, while the ideas are fresh in your mind.

Reading and Writing Assignment

Making Notes from Observations

1. Find and read an article in your newspaper about the outdoors—wildlife, gardening, boating, camping, etc.

2. Tell what the writer has reported as a result of making observations.

3. Tell what additional ideas and information the writer may have gotten by reading.

4. Observe an outdoor occupation or event yourself. Write some notes that would be useful for writing an article about what you have observed.

5. **Optional:**

   a. Write an article about what you have observed.

   b. Be sure you also get some background ideas and information about your subject by reading.

Gathering Facts and Ideas By Listening

Writing Focus...
Listening and Writing

There is a famous line in the Bible that says: "Eyes have they but they see not; they have ears but they hear not."

What this means is that many people see and hear things without trying very hard to understand the meaning of what they are seeing and hearing. For instance, you may hear a great deal about the dangers of drugs and alcohol, about poor health habits, and about highway safety. These things, you say, cannot affect me. A case of having ears and hearing the words but not hearing the message.

One of the most effective ways of gathering information is by listening. This may take the form of an interview where you ask questions and listen closely to the answers. Or, you may get your information at a lecture, from television and radio programs, or form an audio cassette recording.

If you plan to use the information in your writing, you have to make notes as you listen. Because you have done some thinking and planning before starting to gather information, you should have a good idea of the kinds of information you are listening for. This enables you to make notes only about those things that apply to your subject. You cannot use everything you hear in your writing.

If you can record an interview or a program you are listening to, you will be able to listen a number of times to pick up what you want for your notes. The reason for having notes is that you can place them together with the notes you have made from your reading and see how everything fits together when the time comes for writing.

Once again, prepare some questions in advance that you want answered as you listen. In an interview, write down some questions in advance that you want to ask the person you are interviewing. These may not be the only questions you ask, but it gives you a place to start. If you plan on listening to an important speech, write down in advance some questions you hope the speaker will answer.

Gathering Facts and Ideas By Listening

➡ Plan your listening so that you can gather information that applies to your subject.

➡ Pay close attention to what is being said. Listen carefully and thoughtfully.

➡ Make a recording, if possible, that you can refer to later.

➡ Make notes about those things that apply to your subject.

➡ Do not try to use everything you hear.

Listening and Writing

1. Find and read any subject in your newspaper that interests you. This will be the subject for an article you plan to write.

2. Decide how you can learn more about this subject by listening. This may be done by interviewing people and asking their opinions, by talking to someone who is well informed about the subject, by listening to television and radio commentators, or by locating audio or video cassettes on the subject in the library.

3. Listen attentively. Make notes from what you hear.

4. Write an article based on the notes you have made.

Organizing Facts and Ideas 1

Writing Focus...
Organizing Information

By the time you have gathered facts and ideas by reading, listening and observing, your desk may be buried in the notes you have made. Great! You are close to the point where you can start writing with confidence. The job that remains is to put all the information into some kind of order so that you can work with it easily.

Ever since you chose your subject you have been thinking and planning what you will say about it. But as you gathered information, your plans probably changed. Now, as you organize the information, your plans may very well change again. They may change yet again as you begin to write. This is fine.

Eventually a wonderful order will come out of all the changes. Even the best authors go through this process of thinking and changing. It is actually an organizing process. The further you go with gathering information, the more you know about your subject. As you know more and more you can see more clearly what you want to write about first, second, third, and so on.

Your organizing will eventually take the form of a written list of facts and ideas. You write down major facts and ideas in an order in which you think you may use them. Then you add details to each of these major topics. Some writers do this as a formal outline with headings and subheadings labeled A, B, C, 1, 2, 3 and so on. Other writers like to make a "web" or "cluster" of their ideas, like the samples shown on page 29.

However you do it, you eventually will end up with a list that will be the basis of your writing. As you write, you will refer to the list, choosing facts and ideas to write about. But remember, while it is nice to have a list that you can follow, you may find as you write that the order must be changed. It is never too late to rethink and make changes.

8 Summary

Some Steps You Can Follow in Getting Organized

➡ Read through all of your notes.

➡ Make a list of topics you may want to talk about. Leave lots of space between topics where you can add more information.

➡ Go through your notes again. Add information—what you think you would like to tell or explain about each topic.

➡ If you have your notes on note cards or separate pieces of paper, you may find it helpful to divide the cards into piles—one pile for each topic you have chosen to write about. You may even want to discard some of your ideas at this point.

➡ As you go through this process, keep your main subject in mind and think about what you have planned to do with it. The main subject and your main idea about it will serve as the organizing force behind your work.

8 Reading and Writing Assignment

Organizing Information

1. Think about a well-known person, or about some person who is not well-known but who has been in the news lately. Plan in advance what you want to say about this person.

2. Do as much of the following information gathering as you can. Be sure to make notes as you gather information.

   - **Read:** What has been said in newspapers and magazines about the person?

   - **Observe:** Perhaps you have seen your subject in person or on television.

   - **Listen:** What have commentators on the radio and television been saying about the person? What do your friends say?

3. Organize your notes into a list of topics and subtopics that you want to talk about. Rearrange your list until you think you have things in the order you want to talk about them. Then make a final list from which you will do your writing.

4. Write an article about the person.

Organizing Facts and Ideas 2

Writing Focus...
Outlining

There are many different ways to tell a story. What this means is that you can organize your story in different ways. From the moment you select your subject, you automatically think about how you are going to tell it—the order in which your facts and ideas will unfold on paper.

One of the best ways to think of an order for your story is to think how you would tell it to a friend. For example:

Joanne was married yesterday!

After this startling piece of news, you will tell whom she married, how she met the man, and then you may describe the details of the wedding if you know them.

This story is organized by telling the most important fact first and then filling in the details.

I was in an accident yesterday.

In this case, you would probably organize your story in the order that the events happened. This is called a time order or chronological order.

"I was driving north on route 10. When I got to the intersection at Finley Road a car ran the stop sign. I braked as hard as I could but..." and so on to the end of your tale.

Another order is: setting—character—action—meaning or result. You tell where the events take place, who is involved, what happened, when it happened, why or how it happened. To this you might add the meaning of your story—why it is important, or the lessons to be learned from what happened.

Organize Facts By Asking Yourself These Questions

➡ Why am I writing this article? That is, what do I want my readers to find out?

➡ Find the fact or idea you want to start with. Then ask yourself, "What do I want to come next?" Then the next thing, and the next.

➡ Do I want to put things in a time order? Do I want to put the most important idea first and work from there?

➡ What do I want to explain to my readers?

Outlining

1. Find a news article that tells about a situation or an event somewhere in the nation.

2. Read the article carefully. Then make an outline of the article. You can do this by making a list of ideas and facts in the order in which the writer has written them. This is called reverse outlining. That is, the outline has been made after the writing was done instead of before.

3. You can also do a reverse outline with an article you have written yourself. It helps you to see if the order of events and ideas came out the way you wanted them to. Find an article you have written at some other time. Do a reverse outline of the article. Then see if there is a better way you could have organized your writing.

10 *Brainstorming Clusters*

One of the best ways to get a student thinking is through brainstorming. Brainstorming activities can be done individually, with a partner, in a small group, or as a class. Often it's fun for one, two, three, or four students to do a brainstorm cluster and then to share it with the class for comparison.

All you need to do is center or title the paper, board, overhead transparency, etc., with the topic, and around it write all associations that come to mind. At this stage, no association should be discarded. For example:

Newspapers

sports scores	real estate	coupons
classified ads	advertising	fashion tips
comic strips	local news	political news
movie schedules	horoscopes	sun rise time
help wanted	crossword puzzles	recipes
weather	reporters	stockmarket report
advice column	pictures	

Here are some topics you might use:

Front Page

- world leaders
- countries in Europe
- countries in Asia
- countries in Africa
- things taxes are spent on
- kinds of governments
- states and capitals
- names of cabinet members
- names of governors

Local News

- names of surrounding towns
- names of local politicans
- names of local businesses
- names of area restaurants

Sports

- names of sports
- sports teams and cities
- names of players
- sports records
- sports that use a ball
- sports equipment

Classified Ads

- kinds of jobs
- things to sell
- ideal house or apartment

Miscellaneous

- comic strip characters
- warm places
- cold places
- movie stars
- television shows

---

10 *A to Z Lists*

A simply understood way to get into a topic is to cover it from A to Z. This is like a brainstorm, but there is one guideline. Students must find related words according to each letter of the alphabet. These can be people, places, and things connected with the topic, or words to describe the topic.

Because some letters may be impossible to fill, the students can be directed to find a word for twenty of the twenty-six letters of the alphabet. This is a great opportunity to make use of reference books, as students will not solely pull from their own knowledge but from the realm of knowledge at their fingertips.

Here is a sample under the topic "Sports Section":

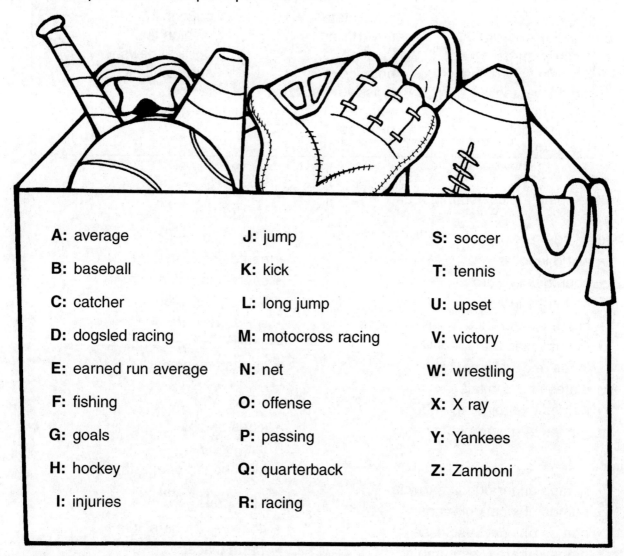

A: average	**J:** jump	**S:** soccer
B: baseball	**K:** kick	**T:** tennis
C: catcher	**L:** long jump	**U:** upset
D: dogsled racing	**M:** motocross racing	**V:** victory
E: earned run average	**N:** net	**W:** wrestling
F: fishing	**O:** offense	**X:** X ray
G: goals	**P:** passing	**Y:** Yankees
H: hockey	**Q:** quarterback	**Z:** Zamboni
I: injuries	**R:** racing	

Any area of the A to Z list, or several areas combined, can now be the focus for writing on the topic. In order to organize thoughts and ideas, maps can be used. A description and sample of these techniques can be found on pages 29 and 30.

10 *"What We Know" Charts*

Another way to brainstorm is to group areas of prior knowledge as well as areas of knowledge the students would like to gain. This type of chart works well with the newspaper. Find an article, and before you read it, complete the chart.

The chart is simple. A paper should be headed "What We Know" on the left side and "What We Would Like To Know" on the right side. As the topic is studied, left side information can be confirmed and right side questions answered.

Here is a sample:

Topic: Baseball

What We Know	**What We Would Like To Know**
• a sport	• How many teams are there?
• 9 innings	• How does a team get to be in the World Series?
• 3 outs	• Who invented baseball?
• 4 bases	• Who has the record for the most home runs?
• 3 strikes you're out	• What team has won the most World Series?
• 4 balls is a walk	• How many teams have never won a World Series?
• 90 feet between bases	
• equipment—gloves, bat, ball, bases	
• two leagues, American and National	

The ideas and questions can go on as long as you wish.

Use the model on page 26 to do your own. It can be duplicated for student or small-group use, or copied onto a transparency for whole-class use on an overhead projector.

10 *"What We Know" Chart Form*

Topic: _____

What We Know	What We Would Like to Know

 10 Surveys

Several sides to a topic can be investigated by conducting a classroom, schoolwide, or take home survey. Opinions held by diverse people can be gathered and grouped, and later analyzed by a student or group in writing.

The class or a small group can plan the questions to be asked that they feel will cover the topic they are studying. The questions should be as unbiased as possible. For example, "Do you feel popularity is a reason why some people are elected to the Student Council?" is a better phrased question than, "Do you think it's fair that popularity is a reason why some people are elected to the Student Council?" Survey questions are phrased for short answers, particularly yes or no. However, because of their restricted form, surveys don't allow for much freedom.

Below is a sample survey that the class can conduct just for fun. Each student gets a response from one adult, one child, and him/herself. Each responder initials the response sheet.

Question	Response
1. Do you subscribe to a newspaper? If so, which one(s)?	
2. What newspaper do you read most often?	
3. How often do you read the newspaper?	
4. What is your favorite section of a newspaper?	
5. Do you use the newspaper to find TV listings?	
6. Do you use the newspaper to find out the weather?	
7. Do you read the comics?	
8. Do you use coupons from the paper?	
9. Do you ever use the index?	
10. How many people in your family read the newspaper?	

After the surveys are complete, gather together in small groups or as a class and pool your responses. Discuss the results and the students' feelings about the results. Share your feelings, too. If you'd like, each student can then do some writing based on his/her findings and feelings about one or more of the questions. Use the form on page 28 to plan your own surveys.

10 Survey Form

Question		Yes	Maybe	No
1.	Person A			
	Person B			
	Person C			
2.	Person A			
	Person B			
	Person C			
3.	Person A			
	Person B			
	Person C			
4.	Person A			
	Person B			
	Person C			
5.	Person A			
	Person B			
	Person C			
6.	Person A			
	Person B			
	Person C			
7.	Person A			
	Person B			
	Person C			

10 Webbing

Whenever a brainstorm is done, it can be placed into a usable format through webs. These are really outlines done graphically. Students can see a blueprint of their writing; they now have the frame on which to build.

Parts of a brainstorm cluster can be linked together according to similarities (although the whole cluster doesn't have to be used). If, for example, a student came up with a cluster like this:

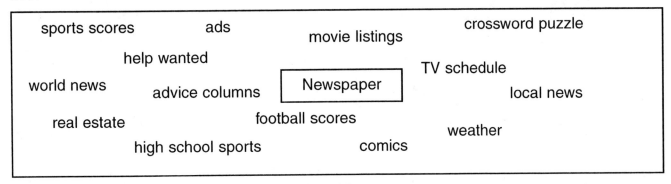

An example of a student's web might look like this:

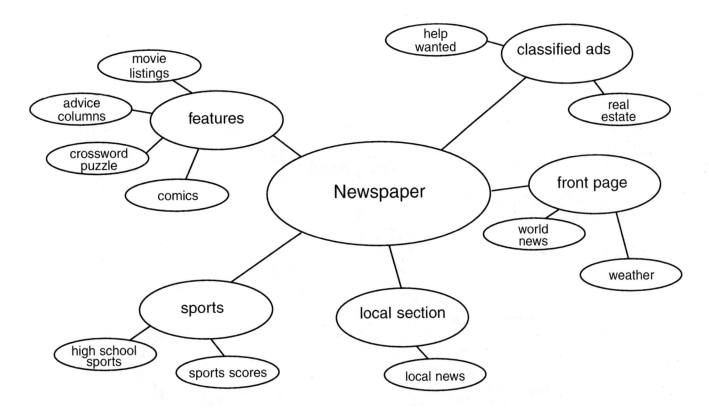

Be sure to model and practice clusters and webs before the students do them on their own. A blank web can be found on page 30.

10 *Blank Web*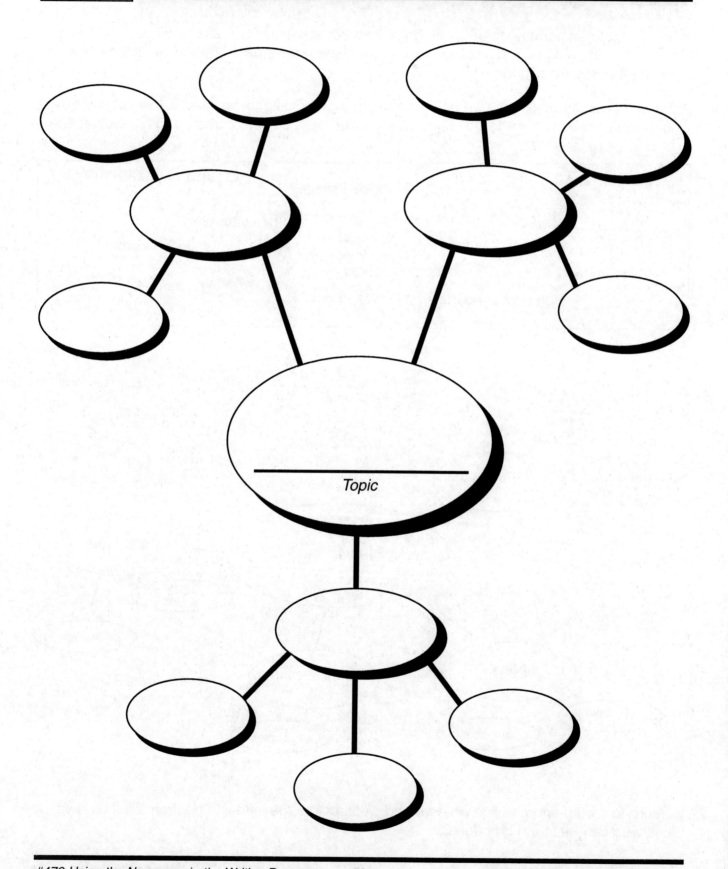

Topic

30

11 *Writing in Journals and Diaries*

Writing Focus...
Starting a Personal Journal

You probably do not remember how you learned to speak. You were too young. But the way it happened was that you listened to others speak and then you tried making the same sounds yourself. At first it was baby talk. But by the time you were three or four you were speaking pretty well.

The same thing happens when learning to speak a foreign language. You listen and imitate. At first you are very clumsy and do not express yourself very well. But as you practice you gain more confidence and the words and sentences flow freely.

Writing is a lot like that, too. When you begin to write you try to imitate the kinds of writing you have read in newspapers and books. But you do not do it very well. The words and ideas come slowly. The more you write, however, the easier writing becomes and the more naturally the words flow from your pen, typewriter, or computer.

One of the best ways to do a lot of writing is to keep a journal or a diary that you write in every day. You are probably most familiar with a diary where you write an account of the things you do each day and what you think about these events.

A journal is a bit different. A journal is used mainly to record thoughts and ideas. These thoughts and ideas may originate in your own head, in your reading, in classes at school, from the media, or in your experiences with people. Most professional writers keep a journal and then refer to it for writing ideas.

It is easy to write in a journal or diary because you are writing for yourself. You do not have to worry about it being rewritten and polished for others to read. But it does wonders for your writing skill. The simple act of writing everyday gives you practice in writing and you become more comfortable about your writing ability. It is the same as practicing speaking. The more you speak the more comfortable you are doing it. There is no trick to keeping a journal or diary. All you need is a notebook full of paper. It can be an old looseleaf binder, a theme book from the school supply section of a discount store, or a colorful blank book that you buy in a bookstore. They all work well if you write every day.

11 *Summary*

Ideas for Keeping a Journal

➡ Set aside the same time each day to write in your journal. Just before bedtime is a good time. Just before starting your homework is another good time. Sometimes, teachers set aside fifteen minutes of class time each day for students to use for writing in their journals. You may want to use part of a study period for your writing.

➡ Write down your thoughts and feelings. Write about something you read in the newspaper. Write about something memorable you heard. Comment on something interesting that you read in a book.

➡ Record the date and where you found the idea you are recording. This will help you find the source of the idea again if you want to use it later as a subject for a story or article.

➡ Try not to skip days. Journals are best when you record ideas that are fresh in your mind.

➡ Have fun with your diary or journal. Do not look at it as a writing exercise but as a friendly conversation with yourself.

11 *Reading and Writing Assignment*

Starting a Personal Journal

1. Browse through an entire newspaper.

2. As you go, jot down notes about anything that interests you.

3. When you have finished, write a page of thoughts about articles you have read. These ideas can be as simple as: "The Cubs won today. It's about time." Or, you might want to go on to explain why you feel it's about time the Cubs won a game. Write enough to fill a page, and more if you want to.

4. Get a book with enough paper in it to continue writing a private journal everyday.

11 *Journal Writing/Free Writing* 👈

Timed (5-10 minute) writing that focuses on content over form, grammar, and mechanics is called "freewriting." It is the best type of writing to be done in a journal. Topics are usually given to the students so that their time is spent in responding to the subject rather than determining what the subject will be. Current events from a newspaper, quotes from a text being read, or a textbook can generate journal topics. A topic that relates to current curriculum studies is useful, but an isolated topic is fine, too.

Here are some ideas:

Things I like to do with my mom/dad...
Something that really makes me angry...
Something that really makes me sad...
Something that really embarrasses me...
A perfect world would...
A good friend is...
I am most like...
I wish I was like...
My greatest talents...
The talents I would like to have...
The most beautiful spot I know...
What my bedroom looks like...
The most horrible sight I ever saw...
My daydreams...
My nightmares...
How I look when I first get up in the morning...
My idea of hard work is...
What I think paradise is like...

The "me" inside that no one really knows about is...
I love to...
I wish I had...
I wish I was...
I am glad that...
My strengths...
My weaknesses...
Am I a...
   ...giver or taker?
   ...doer or watcher?
   ...follower or leader?
   ...peacemaker or arguer?
   ...group person or loner?
I enjoy...
My favorite things are...
My favorite people are...
My least favorite people are...

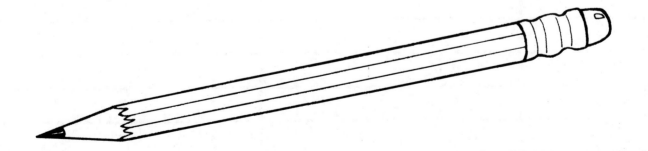

11 *The Person Profile* ☞

Students can use this form while writing in their journals to describe themselves, a person they have read about in the newspaper, a historical or present-day figure, or a fictitious character from literature or their own imaginations. Unavailable information can be hypothesized.

The profile can then be used as a basis for writing.

Person's Full Name: _____

Birthday and Year: _____ Occupation: _____

Full Address: _____

_____

Parents' Names and Occupations _____

_____

Physical Description: _____

_____

_____

Family Description: _____

_____

_____

Home Description: _____

Best Friend's Name and Description:_____

	Favorites	Least Favorites
Food		
Place		
Book		
Person		
Pastime		

12 How to Begin Writing 👉

Writing Focus...
Writing a Lead

You may have noticed that writers use little tricks to lead (pronounced leed) readers into their stories and articles. A very startling or interesting bit of information may be written first. The writer may start with an interesting anecdotal that will be important later on in the article. Or, a problem may be summarized to show readers at once what the article will be about.

Writers use these leads as much to help themselves as to help their readers. It has been shown that writing a lead helps a writer focus on a topic, and it makes the writing that follows easier. That is why some writers will tell you that they spend more time writing good leads than they do writing the entire story.

A lead, in other words, gets you started and gives directions to your entire writing. Here are examples of leads that professional writers have used:

A lead that uses dramatic facts:

> *"A Boeing 727 collided with a smaller plane over San Diego today and crashed in flames to the ground, killing at least 144 people..."* Jim Nichols, *San Diego Evening Tribune*, 1978

A lead that uses emotion:

> *"I will cry a hundred years from now...when I think of what this wind did to my city and its people."* Rich Heiland, *Xenia, Ohio Gazette*, 1974

A lead that uses mystery:

> *"When Diana Oughton, dead at 28, was buried in Dwight, Illinois...the family and friends gathered at her grave did not really know who she was."* Lucinda Franks and Thomas Powers, *United Press International*, 1970

A lead that uses humor:

> *"I ran out in the driveway the other night waving a bag of cold spareribs and shouting to one of my grown kids..."* Erma Bombeck, 1988

It is not easy to think of a good lead. But once it is done, the rest of the article is much easier to write.

Some Ways That Writers Find Their Leads:

➥ Look for leads from the moment you begin to plan your writing. Many writers begin the entire writing process by jotting down possible leads. This helps to find a focus for the story.

➥ Ask yourself questions. What is most important? How does the subject make me feel? What is most interesting?

➥ Brainstorm: Talk to people about your subject. Exchange ideas and feelings. Try woolgathering. This is when you let your mind wander—but have a pad and pencil handy to jot down good ideas that pop into your head.

➥ Write titles or headlines for your article. Titles and headlines often express an important main idea you will be emphasizing in your article. This, in turn, provides ideas for a good lead.

➥ Write and rewrite possible leads. Experiment. Write the first thing that pops into your head. Then, change it. Play with it. Write many possible leads. A good lead is so important that it's well worth the time you spend on it.

Writing a Lead

A "human interest" story is one that involves people (or sometimes animals) and has a strong appeal to your emotions. A disabled person achieves a difficult goal. A dog saves a baby from drowning. A brother and sister are reunited after many years of separation. A poor persons wins the lottery.

1. Find and read several human interest stories in your newspaper.

2. Pay close attention to the writer's lead. How does the writer get into the story?

3. Think of a human interest story you would like to write. It may be something from your own experience or something you have made up.

4. On a separate piece of paper, write many possible leads and headlines for your story.

5. Optional: Write a story that follows from one of the leads you have written.

13 *Creating a Rough Draft*

Writing Focus...
Creating a Rough Draft

You may already be an expert at making rough drafts. If you have been doing your assignments carefully, each of them probably began as rough work. Then you improved on what you did before giving it to someone else to read. But now let's look at the rough draft as an official part of the writing process.

There is nothing that slows down a writer more than thinking that a first effort at writing has to be the last, the neatest and the best effort. Actually, the first effort at writing a story or article is always a rough effort, which is why it is called a rough draft. Some writers even call it "making a mess."

"Making a mess" is a good way to get your writing started. You have done your planning, made a list of facts and ideas, organized them, and you have written a few good leads. This is the time to plunge right in and get your ideas down on paper. Do not worry at this point that what you say is not quite the perfect way to say it, or that it is not neat and pretty. The important thing is getting started.

As you think about what you are writing, you will cross out words and put better ones in their place. You will scribble over whole sentences and write new ones. You will notice where a few words should be added. You make notes to yourself in the margin. But, after a while you have a couple of pages filled with what will become a story or an article. It looks like a mess and it is a mess. It's like a woodcarver's first roughing out of what will be a fine sculpture. At first you see just the rough outlines with bumps and lumps and rough edges. But as the carver works on it with tools and sandpaper, a beautiful figure begins to appear.

Eventually, after smoothing and polishing your rough draft, a well-written article or story will appear that you can be proud of.

Your first job in writing, then, is to get started. Understand from the beginning that your first attempt will be rough and unfinished—a rough draft. Admit to yourself from the outset that this draft will require one, two, or three stages of changing and polishing. This is called rewriting and we will talk about that more in a later lesson.

---

13 Summary

Writing a Rough Draft

➡ Working from your plans, your list of facts and ideas, and your lead, begin to fill pages quickly with your writing.

➡ Expect from the beginning that this is just a first, rough effort that will have to be rewritten.

➡ Make a mess. Change, cross out, rearrange, correct, add words and sentences as you think about what you have written.

➡ Write a second draft that is an improvement over your rough draft. Get used to the idea that you may want to write three or more drafts before you are ready to give your writing to someone to read.

13 Reading and Writing Assignment

Creating a Rough Draft

1. Read a "how-to" or advice column in your newspaper. A "how-to" article tells you how to do something. How to succeed, how to build a table, how to eat properly, how to shop carefully, how to dress fashionably, and so on.

2. Think of something you know how to do well. Or, think of some advice you would like to pass along to others. Make this the subject of an article.

3. Write a rough draft of your article using the tips you learned in the lesson. Make changes in your rough draft as you go.

4. You may want to challenge yourself to see how many pages you can fill quickly with facts and ideas in this first rough effort.

5. When you are finished, reread your draft and make as many changes as you wish.

14 *Writing a Beginning*

Writing Focus...
Beginning a Story

Many years ago, a famous philosopher said that every good story should have a beginning, a middle and an end. "What's so philosophical about that?" you may ask. What he was getting at is that writing should be orderly. The beginning should lead to the middle, which leads to the end. This not only makes it easier for a reader to read, it makes it easier for the writer to write.

This order comes more easily when you have a list of facts and ideas. You recall you made this list during the time you were organizing the information you gathered. You reshuffled the ideas and information until you could see what you wanted to talk about first, second, and so on.

After you have written your lead, look at your list again. The next thing you write about will most likely come from the beginning of your list. And it will begin to explain what you have said in your lead. You can be flexible, however. If the first thing on your list doesn't seem to work well at the beginning, select some other idea to write about first. You can change your list—your outline—as you go.

You must keep asking yourself, however, "Does what I am writing now follow from or go with what I have said before?"

Good writers worry about this all the time they are writing. Then, when they are finished they worry about it some more, and often rearrange sentences and paragraphs to put them in a better order than they were in before. This is one of the decisions you will make after you have written your rough draft. (Rough drafts are discussed in lesson 13.)

Writing the Beginning of a Story

➡ Examine your list of facts and ideas to see if they are in the order in which you want them.

➡ Decide what you want to write about after you have written your lead.

➡ Decide if what you have written begins to explain what you have said in the lead.

The Beginning of a Story

1. Find an interesting article in your newspaper that is fairly long and detailed. Read the article carefully. Use this article as the basis for a story you will write yourself on the same subject.

2. Prepare to write your story. Go through all the pre-writing steps you learned about in lessons 1 through 9: Choosing the subject; thinking and planning; gathering facts and ideas; organizing the facts and ideas; and writing a lead.

3. Write the beginning of your story now and the rest of it in the next two assignments. The beginning of your story should consist of a title, a lead, and one or two additional paragraphs.

4. Rewrite your beginning until you have done the best work you can.

15 *Filling Out the Middle* 👉

Writing Focus...
Writing the Middle of a Story

The middle of your article is where you describe things, explain things you have said, introduce new ideas, and support your ideas with examples and illustrations. In a way, you continue just as you would once you have begun a conversation. The difference is that you continue to work from your list or outline of facts and ideas. This is so that you can stay on track and have a well organized story.

If you have a good outline (your list), and once you have written your lead and the beginning of the article, you will often find your problem is writing too much rather than not finding enough to write about. This is good. Do not worry about saying too much now. You can trim and shorten later.

As you write the middle of your story, you still want to be sure that each thing you write follows what has gone before. Everything you say in your story should be related in some way to everything else.

If you find that something you are writing seems out of place—that it does not "fit" where you have put it—try putting this idea somewhere else. Or, you may want to eliminate the idea altogether.

If you are not sure that all of your facts and ideas are in an order that works well to explain your thinking, make what is called "a reverse outline." To make a reverse outline you reread what you have written and make a list of the ideas and supporting facts as you go. Examine this list to see if each fact and idea is related to ("goes with") what you have said before. And it should all be related to the main idea of your writing.

15 *Summary*

Writing the Middle of a Story

➡ Choose the next item in order from your outline. Be sure each thing you write about follows what has gone before.

➡ When you introduce a new fact or idea, be sure it is related to the main idea that appears in your lead and your beginning.

➡ Keep rereading your work as you go. Ask yourself if you are sure a reader will understand where you have come from and where you are going.

15 *Reading and Writing Assignment*

Writing the Middle of a Story

1. Continue to write the story that you began in the last assignment.

2. Have a conference with your writing coach or with another writer to see if the middle of your story follows and relates to the beginning.

3. Rewrite the middle of your story until you are sure it works the way you want it to. If something seems to be out of order or does not fit where you have put it, see if it will work better somewhere else. If you are not sure, try making a "reverse outline" as described in the lesson.

16 *Writing the End*

Writing Focus...
Writing the End of a Story

When asked what is the best way to end a story, a famous reporter said, "When I run out of ideas, I write THE END."

That's one way to do it, and there is some truth in what the reporter said. When you get to the end of your list of facts and ideas, it's time to stop. However, you might want to wrap things up a little more neatly.

If you have done a good job of focusing your subject, everything in your writing will be related in some way. The most important idea is your main idea. This is the idea that relates all the information and ideas in your story. The ending should also be related in some way to this main idea.

When you have written as much as you think you should, stop and reread what you have said. Look at your lead sentences. Look at your headline or title if you have one. Look at your list of facts and ideas once more.

Then, there are several ways to end your writing gracefully: You may summarize your main idea in a couple of sentences. You may present a final important idea you have been leading up to—a conclusion. A final word of advice to readers may work. A little joke or saying that makes a point is sometimes a good way to end. There is no one way to end a story. You just try various ways until you find one you like.

Here is how two famous stories were ended by their authors:

Merriman Smith of *United Press International* ended his account of the day President John Kennedy was assassinated this way:

> *As our helicopter circled in the balmy darkness for a landing on the White House lawn, it seemed incredible that only six hours before, John Fitzgerald Kennedy had been a vibrant, smiling, waving, and active man.*

Rich Heiland of the *Xenia, Ohio Gazette* ended his account of the deadly tornado that hit his city this way:

> *. . . But we are alive, most of us, although many of us are homeless and must now dig through the wreckage of our dreams for bits of furniture and mementoes, such as a family photo album.*

> *And dig we will. And survive we will. . .*

16 Summary ✍

Writing the End of a Story

➡ First, reread the entire story.

➡ Look at your title or headline and at your lead sentences.

➡ Reread your list of facts and ideas.

➡ Be sure your ending is related to the rest of the story, and especially to your main idea.

16 Reading and Writing Assignment ✍

Writing the End of a Story

1. Write an ending for the story you have been writing during the last two lessons.

2. Before you write your ending, read many stories in your newspaper and see how each ends. Compare the various endings of the newspaper stories. As you read each story, decide how it supports the main idea of the story.

17 A Writer's Tools 👈

Writing Focus...
Using Writing Tools

Every trade has its own special tools and the writing trade is no exception. The first things that come to mind are pencil and paper, a typewriter, and a word-processing computer. If you only have pencil and paper at this point, you can still be a great writer without the technological equipment. Some of the world's largest and greatest books were written by hand. That's where we get the word manuscript—it means written by hand (manus = hand; scriptus = write). Following are some other popular tools of the writer's trade:

A good dictionary is an essential tool for every writer. Ask your writing coach for suggestions. A dictionary is used for many tasks in writing besides looking up spelling or word meanings. Some of the things you can find in a good dictionary include: Pronunciation of words; Synonyms, when you are looking for just the right word to use; Names and dates of famous people; Names and locations of places; Rules for using some words and expressions; Origins of words; To find if a word is too slangy for use in formal writing. A thesaurus helps you find just the right word to describe or express an idea you have. Get hold of a copy of *Roget's International Thesaurus* and ask your writing coach or librarian to show you how to use it.

A general almanac, such as *The World Almanac Book of Facts*, is a tool that fills you in on all sorts of basic information from sports facts to names of members of government, facts about countries, populations, and thousands of other things. Browse through an almanac. You will find lots of short reading about many interesting subjects.

Short encyclopedias help you in a similar way, giving you bits of information on many subjects. They also tell you where to go to get additional information you may need. They are especially helpful in planning articles that contain facts from history, science, geography and biography.

A general encyclopedia is usually the place you start to gather facts and information for your writing. The *Encyclopedia Britannica* and the *World Book Encyclopedia* are two of the best known of the general encyclopedias. (Here's an interesting exercise for a writer: Look in the dictionary to find the Latin and Greek words that the word encyclopedia came from.) In addition to general encyclopedias there are special encyclopedias that deal with special subjects—science, sports, music, history, biography, and so on. Ask your librarian which encyclopedias will be helpful for the subject you are writing about.

The library itself is one of a writer's most important tools. Learn your way around at least two libraries—your school library and one or more public libraries. If you are fortunate to live near a great library, spend some time there. Librarians are very helpful people. Do not be afraid to tell your librarian what you are looking for. You will be given many good suggestions.

17 *Summary*

Tools of the Writer's Trade

➠ Lots of pencils and paper

➠ Typewriter or computer

➠ A good dictionary

➠ Encyclopedias

➠ Books

➠ A journal or diary

➠ The library

➠ A thesaurus

➠ Almanacs

➠ Newspapers and magazines

17 *Reading and Writing Assignment*

Using Writing Tools

1. Spend some time learning how to use one of the writer's tools listed in the lesson.

2. Write an article that tells how this tool can be useful when doing a writing assignment.

3. In your article, use examples to show how the writer's tool can help you with your writing.

18 *Writing Ideas and Activities*

Introduction

There are as many subjects to write about as there are subjects to talk about. In other words, there is no end to the things you may think of for your writing. The following list of ideas is just a start. Do not depend on it for all of your writing ideas. Once you get the hang of working with ideas, it's much more fun writing about subjects you have chosen yourself.

1. You are the manager of a baseball team. Your team has just lost an important game by a score of 10-0. You are explaining to a friend how it happened.

2. You are an elephant watching people in the zoo who are watching you. What are you thinking?

3. Write a one or two-page short story that tells about a day in the life of a tree.

4. You find that by spreading your arms and giving a little jump you can fly. Tell what it's like and what you do.

5. You have been given a million dollars. What will you do with it?

6. You have been granted a wish to be anything or anyone in the world you want to be. Tell what your choice is and how you came to make your decision.

7. Write a four or six-line poem about an animal. Your poem does not have to rhyme.

8. Describe your favorite meal.

9. Describe a natural disaster as if you were an eyewitness—a blizzard, tornado, flood, hurricane, volcano eruption, earthquake, etc.

10. You have just landed on an unknown planet. Describe what you see.

11. Find and read an interesting newspaper article.

    a. Tell what the article is about.

    b. Tell how you feel about what has been said in the article.

12. Look out of the window, either at home or at school.

    a. Describe what you see.

    b. Tell what your thoughts are as you look out of the window.

13. Read several movie reviews in your newspaper. Using these as a model, write a review of a movie you have seen.

14. Select a famous battle from history. You are a war correspondent on the scene. Write an article about the battle for your newspaper.

15. Finish the story that begins this way: "It was a sparkling bright morning when Samantha (or Ben) boarded the big yellow bus."

16. Finish the story that begins this way: "The night was cold, with a strong wind blowing."

18 Story Prompts

Brainstorming

Students can use pictures cut out of newspapers and magazines, or photographs as a basis for writing. Write descriptions of who and what is seen, "What next" predictions, characters' thoughts, personal memories triggered by the scene, or picture captions. To write a story, begin by brainstorming who, what, where, when, why, and how, and then put the pieces together. In small groups, compare the different writings generated from the same picture with the newspaper or magazine articles that the pictures were taken from.

Real Life in History

Everyone has stories to tell. Teach your students to be aware of others and the world around them by tapping into the experiences that others have had. Each student should be assigned to write a news story by talking with one person over twice his/her own age. The student should ask about experiences that person had when he/she was the student's age. Students should delve into the details of what life was like in that particular year, like what people wore, hair styles, fads, what was going on in the world, and what music, television, movies, family life, and school were like.

As a creative extension to go with your social studies curriculum, students can write a news story from the perspective of a person within the time period being studied (like a Forty-Niner or ancient Mayan).

Dear Lois, Love Clark

Students can demonstrate their understanding of a figure from history with this activity based on newspaper advice columns. A favorite historical figure can write a letter asking advice from another person in history. George might write to Martha for advice in keeping his dentures clean. Cleopatra might write for fashion advice.

Editorial Writing Prompts

Making a Difference

Share with your class some copies of editorial pages from various newspapers. Brainstorm what it is that editorials do:

Are they fact or opinion?

Do they tell or persuade?

Are they general or specific?

Are they somewhere in between?

Now, brainstorm some of the students' concerns about world and social issues, like pollution, homelessness, poverty, and war. Small groups with similar concerns can now get together to write an editorial about their chosen topic.

Collect the editorials and publish your own classroom mini-newspaper. Distribute them around the school and to the parents, requesting return "letters to the editors."

Perhaps your class, together with the community, can become involved in solutions to these concerns!

Hieroglyphics

Brainstorm a list of twenty common words, like house, egg, child, and tree. Now have each student create a hieroglyph (a picture symbol that represents a word or idea) to replace each word, similar in style to the ones drawn here:

Once the hieroglyphs are complete, have each student write a story incorporating all of the new words. Exchange the writing among the students. The other students should then try to guess what each hieroglyph represents.

Now have several students come to the chalkboard to share two or three of their hieroglyphs. Compare the similarities and differences between the various creations for the same words. This is a good springboard for a social studies lesson on languages.

18 Story Shuffles

Duplicate pages 51-53 as many times as necessary so that when the cards are cut out, each student can have one from each page. Cut out the cards and place each group in a separate bag, hat, or other container. Students pick one from each container.

These cards indicate the main character, the setting, and the problem to be solved for a short story or news report the students will create.

Take this through the writing process by brainstorming details for each card, webbing, drafting, using a peer response sheet, editing, revising, and publishing the work.

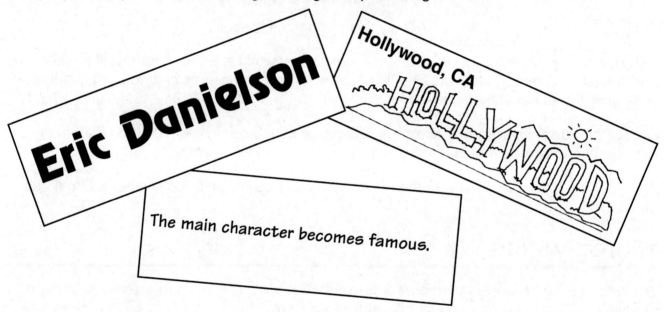

A Perfect World

In one person's perfect world there might be no crime, no war, no money (everyone has everything they need), and pizza and hot fudge sundaes delivered around the clock. What is your perfect world like?

Students will love to brainstorm their Utopia and write a news story about it. They can write what it looks like, what it does, and what it has. They can give it a name, a form of government, and its own system of economics. Students can create these stories in small groups or individually, and then share these with others. Illustrations should be included.

It Made Headlines

Cut out some interesting headlines from several newspapers. Hand them out to students and have them write their own news stories based on the headline. Compare their stories with the original news story.

18 Story Shuffle Cards

The Main Character

A.J. Logan	Ryan Chatel
Danny Kastelic	Erina
Amber Parham	ELSPETH KOHLER
MyLinh Treiu	Brandon Stone
Brianna Holden	Eric Danielson
Timorah Brown	Shaun Bartz
Nicole Fike	Phoebe Steinberg

18 *Story Shuffle Cards* (cont.)

The Setting

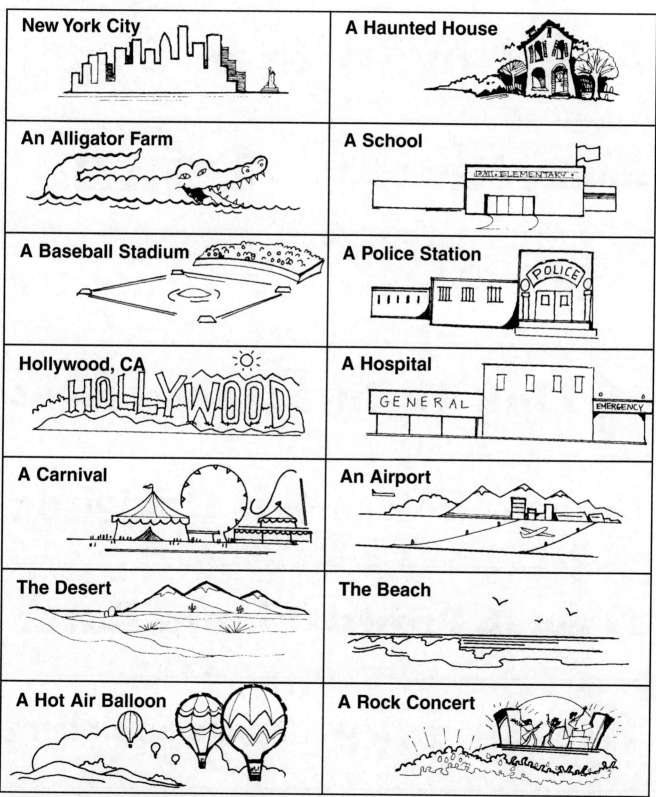

New York City

A Haunted House

An Alligator Farm

A School
PAT ELEMENTARY

A Baseball Stadium

A Police Station
POLICE

Hollywood, CA
HOLLYWOOD

A Hospital
GENERAL   EMERGENCY

A Carnival

An Airport

The Desert

The Beach

A Hot Air Balloon

A Rock Concert

18 *Story Shuffle Cards* (cont.)

The Problem To Be Solved

The main character has the ability to read people's minds.	The main character is trapped.
The main character finds a bag full of money.	The main character is kidnapped.
The main character is being followed.	The main character does not get along with someone.
The main character is lost.	The main character becomes famous.
The main character loses his/her memory.	The main character breaks something valuable to someone else.
The main character suddenly becomes invisible.	The main character wins the lottery.
The main character can predict the future.	The main character can fly.

Descriptive Writing

Character Sketches

Given a character type, it is fun to imagine what that person:

- looks like/wears
- does for fun
- likes to eat
- does for a living

- talks like/says
- smells like
- drives or rides
- lives in (and where)

Create original characters from the following character types. Assign one, or let the students choose from a few or several. It is also fun to create "alter egos" by describing the exact opposite personality. Use the Person Profile on page 34 or just use your imagination!

Day Dreamer	Athlete	Pirate	Beggar
Proud Parent	Toddler	Rock Star	Surfer
Skater	Artist	Detective	Student
Do-Gooder	Teacher	Babysitter	Musician
Snob	Hunter	King/Queen	Teenager

Similar to the above, have students write detailed descriptions for one of the topics at the bottom of this page (or another of your/their choice). In writing, the students should pay careful attention to "sense words"—words that appeal to one or more of the five senses.

You can begin this activity by brainstorming applicable sense word and phrase per sense. For example, to describe an overcast beach scene:

- sight: hazy
- sound: echoing gull cries
- smell: briny
- taste: salty
- touch: damp

These words are now incorporated into the descriptive paragraph(s).

You can use the following as topics if you wish.

- A desert thunderstorm
- Thanksgiving dinner
- Spaghetti and meatballs
- The tooth fairy
- A school cafeteria
- A cozy room

- A Christmas tree
- A dog's bath
- Swimming at night
- A hot summer day
- A public pool
- A video arcade

Writing Focus...
Editing the Work of Others

Editing is the process of reading, correcting, and changing your writing to make it better in many ways. These are the reasons why you edit a piece of writing:

- To correct mistakes in spelling, grammar, and punctuation
- To make your ideas clearer so that readers will understand them better
- To choose better words that express your ideas better
- To rearrange sentences to put them in a better order
- To correct facts that may be wrong

The most important lessons for editing are to make sure that your writing is clear and readable. This means that when you finish editing, your writing should be easier to understand and more interesting for your readers.

Never forget that you are writing for readers and that you are trying to make them understand what you are saying. You understand what you are saying because it's all inside your head. When you take the words out of your head and put them on paper, you have to be sure they are in a form that others can understand.

One way to learn why editing is important is to edit the work of others. When you see the mistakes that others make, you become more aware of trying to avoid these mistakes yourself. When you see that someone else's writing is not as clear and as understandable as it should be, you realize how important it is that you make your own writing clear and understandable.

Editorial conferences are very helpful. In an editorial conference you discuss your work with someone else and exchange ideas on how the writing can be improved. You may have an editorial conference with your writing coach, or you may confer with another writer.

Here is an important point to remember when you are editing someone else's writing: NEVER disparage or make fun of another writer. When making suggestions and corrections ALWAYS start by finding something nice to say. Compliment a good idea, a good attempt, the beginning of a good story. In other words, treat someone you are editing as you want to be treated when your own work is edited.

Editing

➡ Ask yourself if each idea and each fact is clear and understandable. If it's not, ask yourself how things can be changed to make them clearer.

➡ Are the meanings of words clear or can a better word be chosen here and there to make ideas more understandable and more interesting?

➡ Are words spelled correctly? Is the grammar correct? Is the punctuation correct? Grammar, spelling, and punctuation are not simply classroom skills you must master. They are necessary elements for making your writing clear and understandable for your readers.

Editing Letters to the Editor

Option 1

a. Read the letters to the editor in your newspaper.

b. Copy one of them on a sheet of paper. Leave a space between each line so you have room to edit.

c. Make changes in the letter that make it more correct, clearer, and more interesting.

d. Rewrite the letter according to your editing.

Option 2

a. Write a letter to the editor yourself on any subject that you feel strongly about. Others in the class should also write letters to the editor.

b. Edit your own letter and rewrite it.

c. Exchange your rewritten letter with someone else. Edit each other's work. You may prefer to do this in an editorial conference. Then, each writer should rewrite the letter again.

d. Send the letters to the editor of your newspaper.

20 *Rewriting: The Real Secret of Success* 👈

Writing Focus...
Rewriting a Story

It was pointed out in an earlier lesson that many famous writers insist they are not very good writers—BUT, they are great rewriters.

The message of this lesson is short and simple: If you want to improve your writing—REWRITE—REWRITE—REWRITE!

This is the tedious part of writing, but it is very necessary and important. And each rewriting should be preceded by a careful editing job, done by yourself, by someone else, or in an editorial conference.

The question is, "How many times should you rewrite a story or an article?" Unfortunately, there is no good answer to this question. It depends on how much time you have in which to deliver your writing, and it depends on how soon you are proud and happy about what you have written.

Sometimes, when a newspaper reporter is working against a deadline, there may be as little as thirty minutes to write, edit, and rewrite a story. On the other hand, it is not unheard of for an author to spend years writing and rewriting a book. Your rewriting should fall somewhere in between these extremes. When you write an essay question on a test, you may only have thirty minutes to edit and rewrite. If you are doing a term paper, you should start working early enough so that you can edit and rewrite many times. This means starting to work a number of weeks before the paper is due—not the evening before.

The best measure of when to stop rewriting is your answer to the question, "Am I happy and proud to have someone else read what I have written?" If the answer is "yes," you have done enough rewriting. If the answer is "no" or "I'm not sure," read your work once again to see how it might be improved.

Rewriting

➥ Edit your work carefully and thoughtfully.

➥ Consider the advice of others with an open mind.

➥ The most important quality to consider in rewriting is whether your writing is clear, interesting, and easy for your readers to understand.

➥ Decide—honestly—if you are happy and proud about what you have done.

➥ If you can use a word processing program on a computer, rewriting is much, much easier to do.

Rewriting a Story

1. Choose any article from the newspaper that you find interesting.

2. Pretend you are a "rewrite editor" working for the newspaper.

3. Have an editorial conference with another writer in which you discuss the article. Decide what you can leave out of the article, add to it, or rearrange, to make the article clearer and more interesting to read.

4. Rewrite the article to make it better.

58

21 *Clarity: Writing to Be Understood* 👈

Writing Focus...
Writing Clearly

The most important skill you can achieve in either speaking or writing is the same—making yourself understood. This is called clarity.

As a writer, you may make the mistake of thinking that because what you mean is clear to you inside your own head, everyone else will know exactly what you mean. But it doesn't work that way. Others are not inside your head. They can only go by what you write or what you say, so each thing you say has to be absolutely clear before your readers can understand you.

For this reason rules of grammar and punctuation are important. Even a comma, either left out or put in the wrong place, can change the meaning of a sentence. Here is a famous example. Notice how two little commas can make the meanings of two sentences the exact opposite of each other, even though the words are the same:

A woman without her man is lost.

A woman, without her, man is lost.

Another common problem in making yourself clear has the very fancy name of ambiguous pronoun reference. This simply means that people use pronouns—he, her, him, they, them, etc.—without making it clear to readers whom they are talking about. Every writer does this at one time or another:

Bob and Ed were arguing and he looked unhappy.
(Who looked unhappy—Bob or Ed?)

As soon as the men put away their horses, they took a shower.
(Who took a shower—the horses?)

There are so many things that can make speaking and writing unclear that we can not even begin to list them all here. But you can be sure your writing coach or editor will point them out to you as they happen. When it is suggested that something you have written is unclear, do not argue. Your writing coach is one of your readers, and if your writing isn't clear to your coach, it will not be clear to other readers either.

What do you do when something seems unclear? Rewrite the sentence. Use a better word or rearrange the words. There are always many different ways to say the same things and you just have to keep trying different ways until you find an expression that is clear and easy for a reader to understand.

Questions to Ask Yourself About Clarity

➡ Have I written an idea that has to be explained?

➡ Are there facts that might be confusing to a reader?

➡ Is it always clear whom it is or what I am talking about?

➡ Can I make something more clear by improving the grammar or punctuation?

An Emphasis on Clarity

1. Read a commentary-style article in your newspaper. A commentary is simply a writer's comments and opinions on some issue of the day. It may be a commentary in the sports section on how a particular team or league is performing or how the team managers are behaving. It may be a commentary on the country's policies in some part of the world. Or, it may consist of comments about a local or national issue.

2. Write a commentary of your own on the same issue.

3. Edit and rewrite your article as you have been doing.

4. Have your writing coach, editor, or another writer read your finished article for clarity.

5. Rewrite your article once more making clear anything your editor did not understand.

22 A Teacher's Worksheet for Editing

Introduction

The following questions are designed to help teachers prepare for an editorial conference with a student writer. Answers to the questions should be discussed in detail with the student writer, with the writer being an active participant in the discussion. Short, written responses such as "topic not well defined" or "needs development" are counterproductive and will likely be ignored by the student. The writer should be led to make decisions about improvements, rather than be directed to make this or that change.

Conference Questions

1. What is the most pleasing characteristic of the writer's work or style? It is always best to lead off a conference with a compliment.

2. Is the topic well defined and focused? Or has the writer chosen too broad a subject? If the writing does not have a narrow focus, what should be done?

3. Do the elements of nonfiction or fiction exist in the writing? In nonfiction look for such things as facts, arguments, explanations, opinions, and support for opinions. In fiction look for character development, setting, conflict, action, dialogue. In both fiction and nonfiction look for ideas and themes.

4. Have the elements listed above been sufficiently developed? Described? Explained?

5. Are the elements presented relevant to the subject or main idea of the writing?

6. Is there evidence of good organization? If the writing is disorganized, what can be done to put things in a logical order?

7. Is the introduction or lead effective? If not, what needs to be done?

8. Is the conclusion effective? If not, what needs to be done?

9. Is the writing interesting to read?

10. Has the writer addressed the reader's needs—supplied facts, and answered questions a reader may have? If not, what needs to be added?

11. What is the most problematic aspect of the writing? How can it be improved?

12. What two mechanical errors are the most important for the writer to correct? How can the writer learn to correct them? (Two errors are usually the most that student writers can deal with willingly in one conference. To be effective, an editorial conference should center more on a student's thoughts and expression than on mechanical errors. If a student is badly in need of coaching in mechanics, special sessions should be arranged.)

A Writing Partner's Worksheet for Editing

Introduction

One of the best ways to improve your writing is to work with other writers. This can be done most easily when two writers work as partners to read, discuss, and edit each other's work. This following activity can serve as a guide for your discussion during the peer editing stage of writing.

Some writers like to read their work to a partner while the partner listens carefully and makes notes. Other partners prefer to exchange papers and read silently. Either of these procedures works well, or you might want to use both methods at different times during the writing process.

Peer Editing Questions

After reading your partner's work, you may choose to write answers to the questions below, or discuss them orally.

1. What is the title of the work and the author's name?

2. Can you describe the subject of the writing? (Use one or two sentences.)

3. What message, theme, or important idea does the writing express or tell about?

4. What is there in the story that helped make you understand the message or the most important idea in the writing?

5. What ideas can you give your partner that will help to express the message or ideas more clearly?

6. If you could ask your partner only one question about this piece of writing, what would it be?

7. What do you think your partner still needs to work on to improve or develop this piece of writing? (Do not include spelling, punctuation, grammar, etc.) One thing to consider is what more you would like to know about the subject that the writer had not told you. Or, what ideas expressed in the writing would you like to understand a bit better?

8. What suggestion(s) can you make for correcting one or two errors in spelling or grammar that might make the writing clearer? (If you are not sure, check with your teacher, or let it go for now.)

9. What did you like the most about this piece of writing?

22 *Editor's Marks* ✍

After you have written your draft and gotten a response from someone else, edit the draft using these editor's marks. They are the standard marks used.

If you are ready for a challenge, try making up marks of your own!

Proofreading Marks

Editor's Mark	Meaning	Example
	Capitalize	david gobbled up the grapes.
	Make lower case	My mother hugged Me when I came Home.
	Add a period	The clouds danced in the sky
	Spelling mistake	I laffed at the story.
	Reverse words or letters	How you are?
	Add a word	Would you pass the pizza?
	Add a comma	I have two cats two dogs and a goldfish.
	Delete (Get rid of)	Will you call call me on the phone tonight?

22 *Activities*

Modeling

It isn't always easy for writers to learn the concepts of editing and revision. They may know that change is involved and the purpose is to make the writing better, but they may not understand the process. It is important that this process be modeled for them—not just once, but repeatedly with different styles of writing, with writing by different authors (including published authors, you, and them) and in different writing contexts.

Reproduce a short draft of your writing (preferably from an assignment that you are doing with them) onto an overhead or the chalkboard. As a class, discuss the changes in grammar, mechanics, and style that can be made. Make use of the dictionary, thesaurus, and other reference books. Note these changes with colored ink or chalk (if possible, avoid red—it carries negative connotations for the students, and editing should not be seen as negative). Together, revise the work.

Now, provide teams of students (group them in threes or fours) with a paragraph of your writing or anonymous student writing (if you have some from past years or other classes, that is best at this point). Allow the teams to edit and revise onto large sheets of butcher paper or the chalkboard. Share the revisions with the class.

At another time, reproduce a paragraph from the newspaper or the text of a favorite author. As a class or in teams, edit, and revise. If done in teams, compare the results, pointing out the variety of approaches that are possible. (In other words, there is no best way to revise.) Post the originals and the changes around the room.

As part of your regular writing program, now and then do whole class and small group revisions. Make this a natural, expected part of writing.

22 Editing Wordsearch

All of the words in these wordsearches have to do with writing and editing. Do the wordsearch puzzles below by finding the words across, down, backwards, or diagonally. (See page 79 for answers.)

You can also try these suggestions:

- Define the words.
- Group the words that mean "to write."
- Use the words in sentences.
- Make your own crossword puzzle.

```
Q U L T S P E P J M R D F I R
W E R H W D R K G Y X H T A A
L G T R B Y W F N C W H M Y E
M N D E Z I N A G R O M D D L
B I U V O K V C I O A H M U C
C T F I Z T C T H R P C D S O
S S A S X F E S G E B A G L V
T E L I M A K E S S E N S E I
P R O O F R E A D P D N L D M
A E I N M D L P R O O Y U I Z
E T N D H G A R K N T S U T R
I N G N I L L E P S N Q Y I E
R I G H T A U D I E N C E N T
K C N O I T A U T C N U P G B
```

Word Bank

clear	punctuation
draft	response
editing	revision
grammar	right audience
interesting	spelling
makes sense	style
organized	write
proofread	

Word Bank

author	paper
compose	pen
copy	phrase
cursive	poet
dictate	prose
draft	publish
formulate	scratch
indite	scrawl
ink	scrivener
inscribe	stenography
legible	type
manuscript	write

```
D L N T W Q Y E A V P Y F S L O S W E L
I T P I R C S U N A M U D R E S O R P D
C U R S I V E P C M D Q A D G T U C I K
T E O X T M U K P R G J I Y I L Y Q S G
A H K I E B T I A U D R Z W B A V P K W
T K Q N L G P F V Y L O I B L U M I E C
E B E I I J T Y P M W G P O E T R N Y H
U P S S T E N O G R A P H Y S H E D A M
V H E B I R C S N I R L R A P O P I C W
D R E S Q L O R J C C K A S C R A T C H
F O R M U L A T E S S Z S H M S P E K F
F T E W L N C O M P O S E Y T O X D O T
H O A B Y E T O F F Q U W J N T R R G H
R N M T Z R E N E V I R C S U A W H P A
```

23 *Time Capsules* ☞

How will future civilizations remember ours? With this activity students can have a say in just that.

Set-Up

First, the teacher defines "culture" for the class. It is the way a certain civilization lives, the customs it has, the way it dresses, what it eats, its holidays, and its family life. Next, have students read through various newspapers to find several examples that represent today's culture.

Brainstorm

Brainstorm elements of your own culture first. This can be done in small groups, with the findings being shared in the whole group.

Next, brainstorm, as a class, ways in which information about your culture can be stored within a time capsule. (Of course, students will need to know that a time capsule is an enclosed box containing things like current-day newspapers, pictures, music, art, etc., that gets stored and buried to be opened many years later. Students may wish to research the contents of some time capsules, like the ones buried at the New York World's Fairs in 1939-1940 and 1964-1965.) It is a good idea that all suggested ways to prepare the information include writing. Some possibilities are:

- a scrapbook
- a questionnaire of various age group members
- a picture collage with written descriptions
- a videotape of people and places, with scripted dialogue
- a short story that includes many details about modern life in your culture

Finally, as a cooperative group, determine the way you will present your time capsule entry.

Format

As a cooperative group, chart your format with a cluster, map, web, etc.

Writing

Write a draft that includes the layout plan and any illustration ideas. Each student can write a copy of this, or the teacher can reproduce the writing so that each student has a copy.

23 *Time Capsules* (cont.)

Revision

The group will share the comments and revise accordingly. Remember, not all suggestions must be followed. The revisions actually made are always up to the author.

Editing

Using the Editor's Marks on page 63, each student will edit the work alone. The group will then meet to compare and make the corrections.

Complete

The group will write the final draft, and produce the work in whatever form they have chosen. This is a shared activity. Each student is part of a team producing a single product, and they can think of themselves in that way.

Share

The projects will be shared with the class as a whole. Each group can elect a spokesperson or divide the responsibility. What has been chosen, why it was chosen, and why it has been prepared in its format may be discussed.

Storage

All entries for your class' time capsule are ready for storage. To create a ceremony for the "burial" of the capsule, arrange to do one or more of the following (or another you would prefer):

- Bury the entries in a wooden box and mark the spot by planting a tree.
- Present the entries to the principal.
- Present the entries to the school at an assembly.
- Present the entries to the city mayor during a field trip to City Hall.

Make arrangements with a local construction site to have the time capsule buried beneath their building; record this with the city and in the school records.

Note: Some teachers have been known to set a date with the students five, ten, or even twenty years in the future to reopen their capsules. In most cases, at least a few former students remember and meet on the designated future date.

24 Classroom Newspaper

Students can work toward a common goal, improve writing, and have a wonderful time as they produce a class newspaper. Each student can choose the section on which he/she prefers to work, and from those choices the teacher can create small teams to complete the chosen projects. Artistic students might choose to illustrate, persuasive ones to advertise, etc. The door is open for anything, and the following pages can help.

The goal of the class is to create a newspaper. The following steps may be taken, though other steps can be included at the teacher's discretion according to the needs of the class.

- As a class, brainstorm newspaper themes. Some possibilities include: typical newspapers with world news, local news, sports, etc; historical newspapers; school happenings; or family life.

- Choose a theme by classroom vote. (If there are two distinct groups, you might consider producing two newspapers.)

- Brainstorm possible titles for your newspaper. Vote.

- List the following positions for the students. Describe and discuss what each one is and what it does. Descriptions are found on pages 69-73.

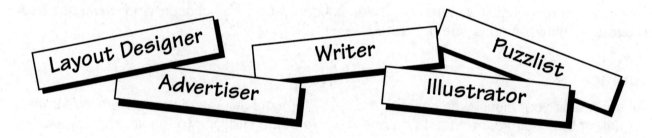

Students choose two sections in which they are interested, indicating with a star their preference. You can then group the students as you see fit, being sure to give them one of their choices.

Although the teacher is the most likely candidate for editor, try to leave the responsibility for the newspaper's production to the students. Let this be their project. They may seek response from one another as well as self and group edit. Revision is a must.

- When jobs are assigned, give each student the appropriate sheet from pages 69-73. This will introduce them to their topic. You can answer their questions and explain as necessary.

- When all work has been completed, duplicate as many copies as you like. Remember to share with other classes and school staff. Be sure to donate a copy to the school library.

Layout Designer

Congratulations! You will design the newspaper from cover to cover. Together with your team you will design where everything goes. You will also decide where to put things on each page. Your teacher will give you a list of all the things that go into the newspaper and how much space each takes. You put it all together, like a puzzle. You will need paper, pencil or pen, and a ruler.

For example, if you have one cartoon that takes ¼ of a page, a poem that takes ¼ of a page, and a feature story that takes ½ of a page, you can lay out your plan

like this:

CARTOON POEM
FEATURE

or this:

POEM FEATURE
CARTOON

or this:

1st half FEATURE | CARTOON
POEM | 2nd half FEATURE

or this:

FEATURE
POEM | CARTOON

There are many other ways to do it, too. You decide! After you plan each page, put the pages in order. Write a table of contents to go on the front page.

24 *Classroom Newspaper* (cont.)

Writer

Congratulations! You will be writing one or more of the pieces for your classroom newspaper. The piece will have to do with your chosen theme and be part of one of the following categories.

- **story**
- **comic strip**
- **poem**
- **interview**
- **feature** (A feature informs the reader about people, products, places, and other things of interest to the readers.)
- **editorial** (An editorial provides an editor's personal opinion about an issue.)
- **"make it yourself"** (A "make it yourself" article gives plans and tips for all kinds of crafts, from origami to cooking to woodworking.)

For example, if your theme is "School Days," you might want to do an interview with the principal, a poem about summer vacation, a "make it yourself" idea on paper airplanes, or a story entitled "The New Kid in School." You and your teacher can decide which category is best for you.

Be sure to follow the writing process when writing. Start by using a pre-writing technique. Follow by writing a draft and getting one or two others to read it and respond. Edit your work carefully, making sure you have said exactly what you want in exactly the way you want. Revise and make a final draft of your writing.

You can also work with an illustrator when writing. Together, plan the artwork for your piece.

Before writing, read articles in some of your favorite newspapers to see how they do it. You can then write an article that copies their style, or better yet, use a style that is all your own.

If you are stuck, or you just need to share your ideas out loud, talk it over with another student and/or your teacher. Good writers know that response from others can only help them to improve.

24 *Classroom Newspaper* (cont.)

Puzzlist

Congratulations! You and the other members of your team are the puzzlists (makers of puzzles) for your classroom newspaper. The class can decide on how many puzzles are necessary. Then you and your teammates can design them. The most typical ones are crossword puzzles and wordsearches (that have to do with your theme, of course) but there are many other kinds to do, too.

Word Puzzles

man	wear	0	he art
board	red	phD	
		BA	
		MA	

(man overboard)   (red underwear)   (3 degrees below zero)   (broken heart)

Cryptics

Cryptics use the next letter of the alphabet in place of the real letter (punctuation stays the same, and "A" follows "Z"):

DBO ZPV HVFTT UIJT QVAAMF?
(Can you guess this puzzle?)

Some cryptics use entirely different letters in place of the real letter (you can either give or not give what the letters stand for.

LQQMYR ML TQOMQHMYR.
(Seeing is believing.)

T=b	M=i	L=s
Q=e	O=l	H=v
R=g	Y=n	

Make Your Own

Create puzzles like this:

 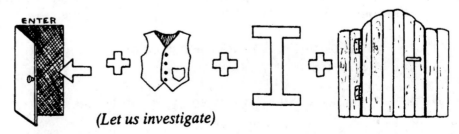

(Let us investigate)

24 Classroom Newspaper (cont.)

Advertiser

Congratulations! You and your team will design the advertisements for the newspaper. Together, you will create at least four original products and an advertisement for each. (The class will decide exactly how many ads to include and how large each will be—full page, half page, quarter page, etc.)

Your products will need to go with the theme of the newspaper. For example, if your theme is "Pets," you might design a dog collar with a radio headset attached, a cat bunk bed, a gerbil amusement park, and chocolate carrots for the rabbit with a sweet tooth.

Once you've created your products, you will need to decide on a slogan for each so that people will want to buy them. For example, the collar radio ad might say "For the Rock 'N' Roll Pup," and the amusement park might declare "It's a Gerbil's Paradise!"

Remember to keep in mind your reading audience—your classmates. The ads should appeal to them. An advertisement meant to get the interest of an adult or a pre-schooler would not be suitable for your newspaper. You are advertising for the newspaper's readers.

Now, put the slogan and product together on an attractive, illustrated, eye-catching advertisement. (You may want the illustrators to help you with the drawing, and be sure to check with the layout team on the dimensions of the ads.) Each of your ads should be neat and appealing. The key is to get people to buy your products.

You probably will not be duplicating your ads in color, so be sure to go over them in dark, black ink so that clear copies can be made.

Note: Before beginning, look at real newspaper advertisements to get more ideas on how to design your ads.

24 *Classroom Newspaper* (cont.)

Illustrator

Congratulations! You will be part of a team for your classroom newspaper. There is a lot of illustrating to do in a newspaper. Remember, you will be drawing pictures in the place of actual photographs. The newspaper needs to have art for each of the following categories:

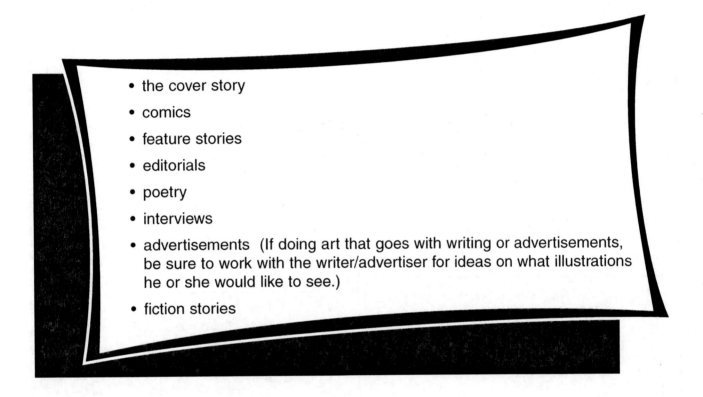

- the cover story
- comics
- feature stories
- editorials
- poetry
- interviews
- advertisements (If doing art that goes with writing or advertisements, be sure to work with the writer/advertiser for ideas on what illustrations he or she would like to see.)
- fiction stories

The layout team can help you decide which size art is best (full-page, half-page, quarter-page, etc.).

It is also a good idea to do rough sketches of your art first before you do the final copy. Since the newspapers probably will not be duplicated in color, it is best to do the art (or go over it) in dark, black ink so that it duplicates well.

Try as often as possible to make your style of art go with whatever it is illustrating. For example, if you are illustrating a funny poem, your art can be cartoonish, but if you are drawing for a serious story, realistic art might be better.

24 Newspaper Pattern

Date

24 *Summary*

Extra! Extra!

The School Times

Room __ News

_____ School Newspaper

Where to Publish

Many magazines and papers publish original student work. Contact the organizations below for details about their current publishing standards and submission requirements.

1. Original responses to fiction or nonfiction can be submitted to:
    The Perfection Form Company
    1000 North Second Avenue
    Logan, Iowa 51546

2. Original writings or art from students grades 7 through 10 can be submitted to:
    Merlyn's Pen: National Magazine of Student Writing
    P.O. Box 1058
    98 Main Street
    E. Greenwich, RI 02818-9946

3. Original writings and artwork from students aged 8 to 14 can be submitted to:
    The Flying Pencil Press
    P.O. Box 7667
    Elgin, IL 60121

4. Original writings and artwork under an assigned theme or topic from students aged 5-9, 10-14, and 15 to no age limit, can be submitted to:
    Cricket League
    P.O. Box 300
    Peru, IL 61354

5. Original writings and art from students through age 13 can be submitted to:
    Stone Soup
    P.O. Box 83
    Santa Cruz, CA 95063

6. Original stories, articles, and craft ideas can be submitted to:
    Highlights for Children
    803 Church Street
    Honesdale, PA 18431

7. Original written and illustrated stories can be submitted to:
    The National Written & Illustrated By...Awards Contest for Children
    Landmark Editions, Inc.
    P.O. Box 4469
    Kansas City, MO 641271993

Writing Certificate

This certificate is to honor excellence in writing achievement to

_____

on _____

_____

Teacher's signature

Letter to Parents

Dear Parents:

The ability to write is as important to a student's success in life as the ability to read. I feel that it is something that all of us should work at together—teachers, students, parents, and as many family members and friends as wish to become involved.

Writing is hard work and we consider the work your child does as serious and worthwhile. The writing done in our class will be shared with you and others as much as possible because we are proud of what we accomplish together.

Here are some suggestions that will help you to help us make your student a better writer as time goes on:

1. Be sure to read the writing your child does. Come to school and read the work that is done here. Always find something to compliment your child about—the ideas, expressions, or feelings. The work you read represents great thought and effort. It will improve with practice.

2. Provide your child with a quiet place to work. Writing is not easy and requires concentration. Writing cannot be done accompanied by music, ball games, television shows, or loud family discussions. If home is not a quiet place to write, your local library is a good alternative.

3. Write with your child. Exchange ideas in notes. Sit down and write the letter you have been putting off for so long. Write to the editor of your newspaper. Start a family history by interviewing older family members and writing down what they say. Encourage your child to keep a diary. Let your child see that you consider writing a useful and important thing to do.

4. Read together with your child and discuss what you read—books, newspapers, magazines. Good writers are always good readers.

5. Never use writing as punishment!

6. The writing process we teach involves rough work and then many revisions. Students edit each other's work and suggest ways it can be improved—just like professional writers do. Try to see to it that your child puts due effort into writing done at home. Read and compliment good ideas. Tell your child that you look forward to seeing the finished work.

7. Have a good, easily accessible desk dictionary in the house for easy reference. Use it frequently yourself to demonstrate that using a dictionary is something everybody does. (A good desk-size dictionary is best. Paperbacks are not complete enough, and large unabridged volumes are too cumbersome to use easily and often.)

Answers to page 65 word searches:

```
Q U L T S P E P J M R D F I R
W E R H W D R K G Y X H T A A
L G T R B Y W F N C W H M Y E
M N D E Z I N A G R O M D D L
B I U V O K V C I O A H M U C
C T F I Z T C T H R P C D S O
S S A S X F E S G E B A G L V
T E L I M A K E S S E N S E I
P R O O F R E A D P D N L D M
A E I N M D L P R O O Y U I Z
E T N D H G A R K N T S U T R
I N G N I L L E P S N Q Y I E
R I G H T A U D I E N C E N T
K C N O I T A U T C N U P G B
```

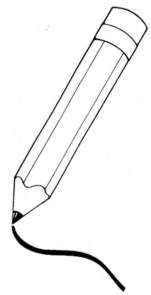

```
D L N T W Q Y E A V P Y F S L O S W E L
I T P I R C S U N A M U D R E S O R P D
C U R S I V E P C M D Q A D G T U C I K
T E O X T M U K P R G J I Y I L Y Q S G
A H K I E B T I A U D R Z W B A V P K W
T K Q N L G P F V Y L O I B L U M I E C
E B E I J T Y P M W G P O E T R N Y H
U P S S T E N O G R A P H Y S H E D A M
V H E B I R C S N I R L R A P O P I C W
D R E S Q L O R J C C K A S C R A T C H
F O R M U L A T E S S Z S H M S P E K F
F T E W L N C O M P O S E Y T O X D O T
H O A B Y E T O F F Q U W J N T R R G H
R N M T Z R E N E V I R C S U A W H P A
```

Bibliography

References and Resources

Anderson, Richard C., Elfrieda H. Hiebert, Judith Scott, and Ian A.G. Wilkinson. *Becoming a Nation of Readers.* Center for the Study of Reading, 1985

Atwell, Nancy. *In the Middle: Writing, Reading and Learning with Adolescents.* Heinemann, 1987

Bettelheim, Bruno. *The Uses of Enchantment: The Meaning and Importance of Fairy Tales.* Knopf, 1976

Caplan, Rebekah. *Writers in Training: A Guide to Developing a Composition Program for Language Arts Teachers.* Dale Seymour Publications, 1984

Cullinan, Bernice E.,ed. *Children's Literature in the Reading Program.* International Reading Association, 1987

Eidenier, Connie Wright,ed. *1990 Children's Writer's & Illustrator's Market.* F & W Publications, 1990

Graves, Donald and Virginia Stuart. *Write from the Start.* Dutton, 1985

Graves, Donald. *Writing: Teachers and Children at Work.* Heinemann, 1985

Sebranek, Patrick, Dave Kemper, and Verne Meyer. *Write Source 2000.* Write Source Publishing House, 1990

Melton, David. *Written and Illustrated by...* Landmark Editions, Inc. 1985

Murray, Donald. *Read to Write: A Writing Process Reader.* Holt, Rinehart and Winston, 1984

Murray, Donald. *Writing to Learn.* Holt, Rinehart and Winston, 1984

Rice, Dona Herweck. *Write All About It!* series. (TCM 500-503) Teacher Created Materials, Inc., 1993

Silberman, Arlene. *Growing Up Writing: Teaching Children to Write, Think, and Learn.* Times Books, 1989

Learning ™ P.O. Box 54293, Boulder, CO 80322–4293

Robertson, Deborah and Patricia Barry. *Super Kids Publishing Company.* Teacher Ideas Press, 1990

Computer Software Programs

Bank Street Writer for the Macintosh. Scholastic, 1991.
Davidson's Kid Works 2. Davidson, 1992.
My Own Stories. MECC, 1993.